Bryce Courtenay

INTRODUCES

The Australian History
~ Collection ~

The Five Mile Press

The Five Mile Press

The Five Mile Press Pty Ltd
22 Summit Road
Noble Park Victoria 3174
Australia
Originally published as eight separate books
for Cadbury Schweppes Pty Ltd in conjunction with Kidcorp Pty Ltd

First published in this format 2001

Cover design: Geoff Hocking
Introductions: Bryce Courtenay
Stories: Sonya Plowman and Maggie Pinkney

National Library of Australia Cataloguing-in-Publication data
Bryce Courtenay introduces the Australian history collection
ISBN 1 86503 480 0
1. Australia - History – Juvenile literature. I. Hocking, Geoff. II. Forss, Ian. III. Title.
994

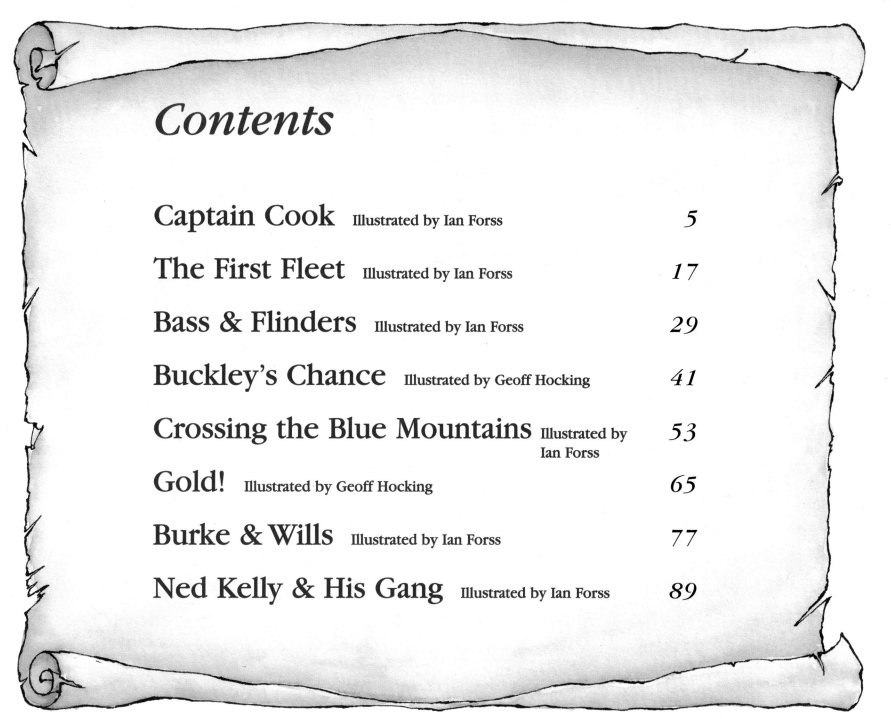

Contents

Life was tough during Australia's first 100 years of European settlement. But some pretty exciting things happened too – as you'll see from these eight true stories.

It all started when Captain Cook landed at Botany Bay. Everybody knows he was a great explorer but very few people know that he also discovered lemon juice. He wasn't the first person to squeeze the juice from a lemon, but he found out that lemon juice stops sailors getting scurvy. (Scurvy is caused by a lack of vitamin C – it rots your gums and then all your teeth fall out!)

Most older sailors in those days had no teeth – until Captain Cook took lemons along with him on the voyage to Australia. That fixed the problem. It's not such a big thing as exploring foreign lands, but if you were a sailor you'd be pretty grateful.

One more thing. Did you know that up until the 20th century most people were much smaller than they are today? This is because they didn't get enough good food. You can see how small they were if you go and see Captain Cook's cottage in Melbourne's Fitzroy Gardens. It was brought out from England, stone by stone, many years ago.

Captain Cook

Long ago, in 1728, a lad named James Cook was born in the north of England. James was destined for life on the sea and at age 18 he took up his first job on a ship. Later he joined the navy and became so well-respected for his seamanship that he was chosen to lead an expedition aboard the HMS *Endeavour*.

This expedition was a very important one. Firstly, astronomers needed to travel to the southern hemisphere to make some valuable scientific observations. And secondly, a mysterious 'great southern land' was thought to exist in the Pacific Ocean. Cook set out to see if he could find it.

The *Endeavour* was a fine vessel over 32 metres long, carrying more than 90 crew and passengers. Amongst all the passengers were Joseph Banks, a respected botanist, and two artists whose job it was to draw the people, landscapes and animals they saw on the voyage.

Tonnes of supplies were taken on board to see the crew through their long journey. The food included oatmeal, vinegar, beer, rum, sauerkraut, pickled beef and pork, orange and lemon syrup, and plenty of water.

The ship also carried sheep, pigs, chickens, a goat and a cat. The goat was on board to supply the crew with fresh milk. It was an experienced sailor, having already completed one journey around the world.

When everything was stowed on board it was
at last time for the exciting voyage to begin!

they spotted New Zealand, which had already been discovered. Cook and his crew spent six months exploring the coast, and learnt that the country was actually composed of two islands, not just one as originally thought.

On the last day of March 1770, the *Endeavour* left New Zealand. Less than three weeks later land was sighted again, and this time it was the east coast of Australia!

The *Endeavour's* first stop was Tahiti, where the astronomical measurements were taken. Captain Cook then sailed south in search of the legendary fabled 'great southern land'.

They sailed and sailed, but they found no great southern land. Then one day — land ahoy! —

Their first landing spot, at the end of April, was a bay lined with a beautiful white beach. The crew feasted on the huge stingrays they found in the clear blue waters of the bay.

Cook initially named this place Stingray Harbour, but later changed it to Botany Bay, due to the abundant plant life there.

Joseph Banks was beside himself with excitement about the vegetation that he was able to collect and study — it was so different to that found in his homeland!

The Europeans weren't the only people to have found this bay. There were many Aborigines already living there, and they wanted the newcomers to leave.

Cook's crew gave them beads and mirrors and other tokens of friendship but the Aborigines found no use for them and threw them away. They threw spears at the intruders and ran away to hide.

Cook stayed in Botany Bay for a week, exploring the countryside and loading up with fresh food supplies.

Then Cook decided to set sail for the north. But they weren't long out to sea when trouble suddenly struck. The *Endeavor* had snagged itself on the Great Barrier Reef!

Disaster! All hands on deck! A thunderous sound was heard as the waves burst against the ship. The ship's wooden planks were ripped open by the sharp coral reef, and water gushed in around Cook's feet.

Working furiously, the crew threw forty tonnes of supplies overboard to lighten the ship's load. Firewood, guns, cannons, barrels — the men had no choice but to throw them into the sea. Everyone worked desperately to bail the water out of the leaking ship.

13

Once the ship had been fixed they sailed up the coast to Cape York, where Cook named the entire east coast New South Wales.

He then began the long voyage back to England via New Guinea, Java, and the Cape of Good Hope.

Throughout the journey, Cook had wisely made sure that his crew ate fresh fruit and greens to prevent them from becoming ill with scurvy. Tragically, however, almost half the crew died on the return voyage, mostly from malaria picked up in Java.

Finally, after hours of back-breaking work, all was well and the *Endeavour* was beached for repairs.

Over the next few months, the *Endeavour* sailed through seemingly endless waters. Sometimes it seemed they would never reach their homeland. And then one day they saw a little speck in the distance, and then the speck turned into land ... and by July 1771 England was in sight!

Everybody was ecstatic. Some of them had left behind wives and children, and longed to be reunited with their families. Each passing day brought them closer and closer to England.

After a journey of almost three years, the *Endeavour* had finally made it home.

How would you feel if you were suddenly told you were being sent to the moon, and that you'd never see your family again? Not too happy, huh?

The convicts of the First Fleet must have felt the same way. They were packed into leaky boats and sent to an unknown land on the other side of the world.

They were locked in smelly dungeons below deck, which they shared with rats and cockroaches. Gross! The food was stale, and there was never quite enough. At first the convicts were too cold because they didn't have many warm clothes, but once they reached the tropics it was sweltering down there – and the smells got even worse. It's a wonder anyone arrived alive!

When they first saw a kangaroo they thought it was a giant rat. (As if they hadn't seen enough rats already!) They'd come to a land even stranger than the moon, where the rats were as big as ponies. Help – GETMEOUTTA-HERE!

Mind you, the Aborigines at Botany Bay must have got a big shock too. Suddenly something that looked like a huge white bird sailed into the harbour, and then a lot of scary-looking 'ghosts' came ashore. And the horses, goats and pigs probably looked just as strange to the Aborigines as the kangaroos did to the convicts!

And why did the white people start chopping down trees the minute they arrived? The Aborigines had lived in Australia for 40,000 years or more – and in that time they had hardly made a mark on the landscape. But things were about to change – and fast!

BRYCE COURTENAY

The First Fleet

By the end of the eighteenth century, England's cities had become filthy and overcrowded. The poor lived in grimy, tumbledown slums, and life was very harsh. Many people were out of work, and so they were forced to choose between starving to death or begging and stealing.

If they were caught they could be imprisoned – or even hanged – just for stealing a loaf of bread. All the gaols soon filled up, so many convicts were shipped off to the British colonies in America to serve their sentences. This was called transportation.

But transportation to America stopped in 1776 when the Americans fought against the British and won their freedom.

So the British had to find somewhere else to send their criminals. At first, old ships on the Thames were used as temporary gaols.

A new dumping ground for Britain's convicts would have to be found. Sir Joseph Banks, the botanist who had accompanied Captain Cook on his Pacific voyages aboard the *Endeavour*, suggested establishing a prison settlement in far-off Botany Bay.

There were no dangerous animals, the climate was mild and the soil suitable for farming, he said. Before long the colony would be able to support itself.

The English wanted a base in the Pacific, fearing the French or Spanish would beat them to it. Starting a penal colony in an unknown land was a bold move. But it would solve the problem of the overcrowded gaols and enlarge the British Empire at one stroke.

The British government decided to establish a settlement at Botany Bay. The man put in charge of this huge project was Captain Arthur Phillip, a 49-year-old naval officer and farmer. He was appointed Governor of New South Wales.

But these half-rotted, rat-infested ships only provided a short-term answer. Before long they were crammed to overflowing, and still more convicts were arriving daily.

Diseases of all kinds were rampant and, with the help of rats, they soon spread throughout the hulks – killing hundreds of prisoners.

The authorities of the day were heartless by modern standards, but even they realised something had to be done – and done quickly.

It took two months to load the storeships of the First Fleet for the long voyage. Enough food had to be packed to last the new settlers for two years. After this, the British government hoped the colony's own crops would be ready for harvesting. Seeds and plants for growing in the new colony were carefully packed into the hold.

Tools and materials for clearing and farming the land and for building houses also had to be packed. But the government wanted to keep costs down, so they didn't provide enough food or clothing for the convicts. There was not even enough ammunition for the guns. Captain Phillip, fearing a convict riot, kept very quiet about this.

The wives of many of the convicts came down to Portsmouth to say goodbye. There were noisy scenes as some of the wives begged to be taken with their husbands. But this was not allowed.

In the early hours of Sunday 13 May 1787, the First Fleet sailed quietly out of Portsmouth on its long voyage. Jammed into the six transports were about 770 convicts, including thirteen children.

The fleet consisted of eleven ships altogether. As well as the transports, there were three storeships and two naval vessels: the *Sirius*, under the command of Governor Phillip and the *Supply*. Other people aboard included officers, marines, members of the ships' crew and a handful of administrators and their wives and children.

The convicts had no idea of what to expect when they arrived at Botany Bay. For some of them it seemed like an adventure at first, but they were confined below decks and soon became very bored and miserable. Fighting often broke out. Conditions were almost as bad as on the hulks on the Thames – the air was stale, there wasn't enough food and the transports were infested with rats and cockroaches. But luckily the seas were calm for the first part of the voyage.

After stopping at the Canary Islands to take on fresh fruit, meat and vegetables, the fleet reached Rio de Janeiro in early August. Here the ships anchored for a month.

They were cleaned and repaired and more fresh supplies were taken aboard. Boatloads of oranges were given out each day.

Setting sail from Rio de Janeiro on 4 September, the fleet struck wild seas as it crossed the southern Atlantic Ocean for the Cape of Good Hope.

Convicts and crew alike suffered from terrible sea-sickness and must have feared for their lives as the small wooden ships were lashed by towering waves.

In October the fleet arrived in South Africa and spent another month in Cape Town. Again, the ships were cleaned and repaired and fresh supplies of food were brought in.

Shortly before the ships sailed for Botany Bay, livestock of all kinds was loaded aboard, including bewildered sheep, cattle, pigs, goats and hens. Now the fleet was ready to embark on the longest leg of the journey.

Captain Phillip, in an advance party, rounded Van Diemen's Land (now Tasmania) and arrived at Botany Bay on 18 January. But he was disappointed by what he saw.

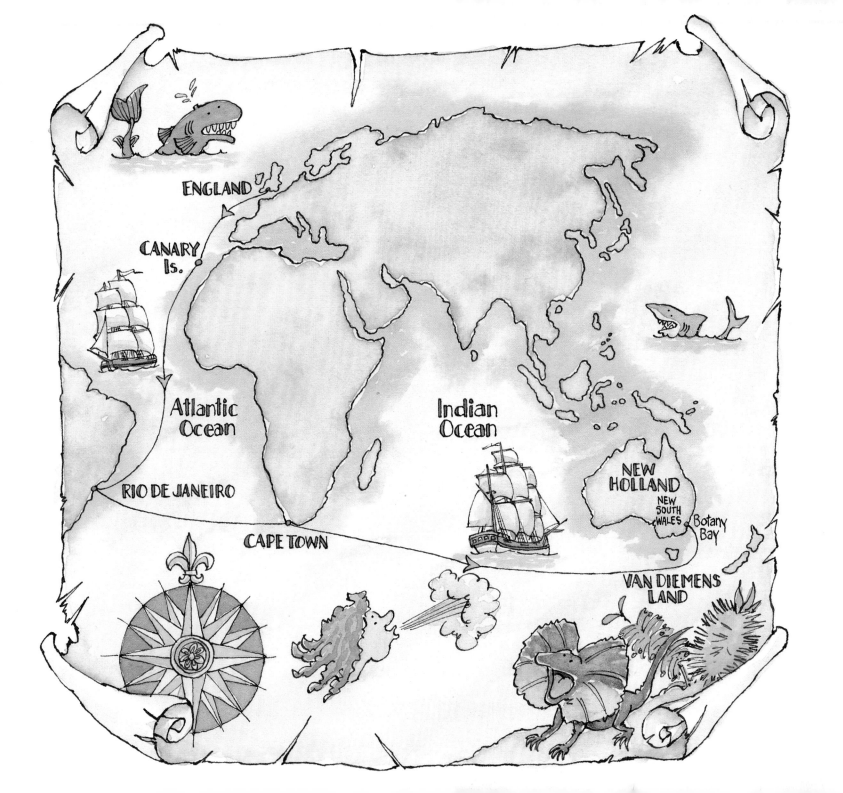

ENGLAND

CANARY Is.

Atlantic Ocean

RIO DE JANEIRO

CAPE TOWN

Indian Ocean

NEW HOLLAND

NEW SOUTH WALES

Botany Bay

VAN DIEMENS LAND

The bay was too shallow, the soil was sandy and there wasn't enough fresh water. So he sailed further north till he found the magnificent deep, sheltered harbour of Port Jackson. Here the entire fleet anchored.

On 26 January 1788 a group of marines and convicts from the *Supply* went ashore at a pleasant cove, later named Sydney Cove. They raised the British flag, and drank toasts to King George and the success of the new colony.

Eight months after setting out from Portsmouth, the First Fleet had at last arrived. But not everyone had lasted the distance. About forty people had died at sea, and many others were seriously ill.

The peaceful shores of the cove soon rang out with the sound of axes as trees were felled and the land cleared. Tents were erected and cooking fires were started. When this was done the sick were brought ashore and treated. A blacksmith's forge was set up.

All this activity was watched from afar by the indigenous people who had lived peacefully here for many thousands of years. From the white settlers' point of view there was still a great deal to be done. The task of clearing the densely-wooded land, building houses and roads, and eventually growing enough crops to feed the colony seemed an almost impossible task. And yet the first great step had been taken. It was a turning point in the future of this ancient dreaming continent. Things would never be the same again.

Bass and Flinders were pretty important because they were the first people to discover that Tasmania wasn't joined on to the rest of Australia. This mightn't sound like a very big discovery, but it meant that ships could cut a whole week off their voyages between England and Australia. After months at sea, I'm sure you'd be keen to walk off the gangplank a week earlier!

A young servant boy called William Martin went with them on their first voyage. The three of them sailed around Botany Bay in a tiny rowing boat called the *Tom Thumb*, which Bass had brought out from England.

Then Flinders mapped the whole of Australia by sailing into every little nook and cranny on the coastline. Before that, people had only had a vague idea of how Australia was shaped.

Matthew Flinders had a special mate, his cat Trim, who sailed with him. When they came ashore Trim would go on land and disappear, but the night they were due to sail Trim always appeared just in time. Some cat, hey?

Although he's famous today, Flinders never got much reward or recognition for his great achievements during his short lifetime.

Did you know that Flinders was the person who first suggested calling this country Australia? It means 'south'.

BRYCE COURTENAY

Bass & Flinders

When Matthew Flinders was a boy in England he read *Robinson Crusoe*. From that time on his head was filled with dreams of exotic desert islands and faraway places. He longed to go to sea. At the age of 15 he became a lieutenant's servant on the sailship *Alert*. There he learned about sailing and daily shipboard life. He also studied mathematics, astronomy and navigation.

George Bass, who was three years older than Flinders, was a doctor. He too had a love of ships and the sea, and a longing to see exciting new places.

In 1794, the two young men met aboard the *Reliance*, which was taking Governor Hunter to Sydney. Bass, aged 23, was the ship's surgeon, and Flinders, now 20, was an officer. During the long voyage they had the chance to talk about their shared dreams and ambitions. Soon they became firm friends.

Bass wanted to do some exploring when he arrived in Australia, so he had brought with him a small rowing boat, the *Tom Thumb*. He had also hired a young servant, William Martin, to help him on his voyages. Flinders said he would like to go with them. The *Reliance* reached Sydney in September 1795.

Governor Hunter was most impressed when he saw their work. The colony was in desperate need of accurate maps of the surrounding coastline, and he felt that Bass and Flinders were just the men to provide them. Hunter ordered that a larger boat be built for the two explorers – the *Tom Thumb II*.

A few weeks later, Bass, Flinders and Martin set off in the *Tom Thumb* to explore the coast-line of Port Jackson. They sailed through the Sydney Heads in the tiny rowing boat and south past the deserted beaches (later known as Bondi and Coogee) to Botany Bay and the Georges River. The return trip took nine days. During this time they made very accurate maps of the coast.

The following year, Bass and Flinders used the *Tom Thumb II* to explore the coast south of Botany Bay. They discovered Port Hacking and sailed south as far as Lake Illawarra.

At one stage, they nearly lost their lives in a gale. But luckily they were able to take shelter in an inlet which they named Providential Cove.

Late in 1797, Governor Hunter put Bass in charge of a whaleboat and six oarsmen, instructing him to sail down the coast as far south as he could. Flinders wasn't able to go on this voyage. Bass followed the coastline, sailing westward at Cape Howe until he came to Wilson's Promontory. He sailed around this and continued west, where he discovered Philip Island and Westernport Bay.

On their return, bad weather forced the party to shelter at Sealers' Cove on Wilson's Promontory. They were running short of food so they killed some seals and smoked the flesh.

In October 1798, the *Norfolk* sailed out of Sydney Heads and down the coast to the south. After waiting some time for heavy gales to clear the explorers eventually sailed west through the strait, at last proving its existence. They now knew that all the existing maps were wrong! Then they sailed right round Van Diemen's Land and back to Sydney.

While rounding Wilson's Promontory, Bass observed south-westerly currents. This made him suspect that there was a strait of water between Van Diemen's Land (Tasmania) and the mainland. Up until then, navigators had believed that Van Diemen's Land was joined to the rest of the continent.

When Bass returned to Sydney he reported his hunch to Governor Hunter. The governor put Bass in charge of a small ship called the *Norfolk*, and a crew of eight. This time Flinders was able to go too. Hunter instructed them to look for a strait, sail west through it (if it indeed existed) then circumnavigate Van Diemen's Land before returning to Sydney.

TASMANIA

Sadly, this successful voyage was the last that the two friends made together. Bass left the navy and bought a ship called the *Venus* to become a sea trader. In 1803 he left Sydney aboard the *Venus*, heading for Chile.

What happened to him after that remains a mystery. He, his ship and crew disappeared without trace. It is thought that Bass may have been captured by pirates and either killed or set to work in South American silver mines.

When Bass and Flinders reported their news to Governor Hunter he was delighted. He immediately named the newly-discovered channel of water Bass Strait. This was an important discovery because it meant that ships could sail through the strait instead of rounding the south of Van Diemen's Land – cutting the journey from England to Australia by about a week.

In early 1801, Flinders married Ann Tyler. He sought permission for her to come to Australia with him but this was refused. So in July 1801 Flinders set sail in the *Investigator* without her. It was to be many years before they would see each other again.

Flinders returned to England in 1800, where he wrote a book about his voyages of discovery in Australia. He dedicated it to the famous botanist Sir Joseph Banks. Banks used his influence to have Flinders promoted to captain and put in charge of a warship, the *Xenophon*. This was refitted and renamed the *Investigator*.

The *Investigator* reached Cape Leeuwin, the south-west tip of Australia, in December 1801. From here Flinders continued eastward along the south coast of the continent. He was amazed at the towering cliffs of the Great Australian Bight.

After exploring and charting the Spencer Gulf and the Gulf of St Vincent he went on to sail around the whole continent, doubling back along southern Australia and finally arriving in Sydney in June 1803. He had made history as the first captain to circumnavigate Australia.

By the time Flinders was released his health was broken. Only 36 years old, he was gaunt and weak. The day that his book was finally published, in July 1814, Flinders lay dying. His wife Ann pressed a copy of the book into his hands but he had lost consciousness. He died the next day, aged only 40 – a sad end for a brave man who had made such a huge contribution to the exploration and mapping of the Australian coastline.

After this Flinders was beset by bad luck. In September 1803 he set off for England in a ship called the *Cumberland*. It began to leak so badly that he was forced to stop at the French-controlled island of Mauritius to have repairs done. What Flinders didn't realise was that England and France were at war. The French thought Flinders was a spy and immediately put him in prison. There he remained for the next seven years. He used his time to write *A Voyage to Terra Australis*. In this book he made the suggestion that the newly-settled continent be called Australia.

It's strange how expressions get into the language. 'Buckley's chance' is an example. It means you have almost no chance at all.

Buckley was one of three convicts who escaped and fled into the bush. They soon discovered that the bush was even more hostile than prison, so two of them gave themselves up. But Buckley reckoned he'd rather die than go back to chains.

Well, he got lucky when a tribe of Aborigines decided he was the spirit of a Dreamtime elder, and looked after him. With their help he survived. There was about a chance in a million of that happening, so that's where we get the expression, 'Buckley's chance'.

Buckley didn't meet another Englishman for thirty-two years, so when he finally bumped into some fellow countrymen he had almost forgotten how to speak English!

The tale of Buckley's lonely exile is one of the strangest – and saddest – in our early history. Imagine how he felt when he saw his ship, the *Calcutta*, sailing out of the heads all those years ago! Maybe be wished right then that he'd given himself up like the other two.

BRYCE COURTENAY

Buckley's Chance

With the arrival of the First Fleet in 1788, the British claimed the whole of eastern Australia, calling it the Colony New South Wales. Despite this, the British were alarmed by reports that French ships were snooping around southern Australia. Fearing that the French were planning to establish a colony of their own, Britain decided she had better quickly set up a second settlement. This was to be at Port Phillip Bay.

Lieutenant-Colonel David Collins, who had accompanied Governor Phillip in the First Fleet, was given the task of setting up the new colony. In 1803, a transport, the *Calcutta* and a store-ship, the *Ocean*, set sail for Port Phillip Bay.

Three hundred convicts, specially chosen for their building or farming skills, were aboard the *Calcutta*. Among them was William Buckley, a cheerful young giant of a man from Cheshire. He had worked as a brick-layer before joining the British army.

As a soldier he had fought bravely against the French in Holland, and he was well liked by his commanding officers.

But in 1802 he was convicted of stealing a bolt of cloth, and was sentenced to life imprisonment with hard labour in the new colony.

On 9 October 1803, the *Calcutta* and *Ocean* sailed into Port Phillip Bay and anchored at what is now Sorrento. The convicts were set to work clearing the scrub and building shelters while the marines explored the area.

Lieutenant Collins soon realised that the sandy, windswept soil wouldn't be suitable for growing crops. He reported to Governor King in Sydney that the area was unsuitable for settlement. Governor King gave him permission to move the colony to Van Diemen's Land.

When they heard this news, four convicts – including Buckley – decided to escape. Perhaps they hoped to reach the settlement at Sydney Cove, not realising how far away it was.

The men managed to steal boots and food in preparation for their escape. Two nights later they slipped out of the camp. But a sentry heard them and raised the alarm.

Now the chase was on! Buckley and his companions rushed through the tea-tree scrub with several armed soldiers chasing after them.

One man was shot and captured, but the other three escaped into the bush.

Eventually they could see the *Calcutta* across the curve of the bay. By this time, two of the men were thoroughly sick of life in the wilds. They lit a fire in the hope that someone from the convict camp would row over and rescue them, but after waiting a day they realised their signal hadn't been seen. So they wearily retraced their steps around the coast and gave themselves up. Buckley refused to go with them.

They were free at last! But what had they got themselves into? Everything was so strange and different from the peaceful English countryside they were used to. Hearing the eerie nightcalls of the bush, they must have begun to wonder if escaping had been such a good idea after all. Who knew what strange wild animals roamed the bush, or how the native people would treat them? And what would they live on?

Rather than going into the dense bushland, the three men decided to walk along the shore. At least the sea was familiar. When their rations ran out they ate shellfish and wild berries. Their main problem was finding enough fresh water.

45

Several days later Buckley saw the *Calcutta* and the *Ocean* sail out of the narrow heads into Bass Strait. Now he was all alone!

He realised he must find fresh water if he was to survive. After stumbling along the shore for a few more days he came across a coastal stream shaded by overhanging trees. Footsore, thirsty and suffering from sunstroke, the exhausted Buckley decided to rest there until he had regained his strength. Luckily, shellfish and wild berries were plentiful.

One day Buckley was startled to look up and find three Aborigines staring down at him. They seemed friendly, but Buckley wasn't sure what their intentions were. As soon as they had gone he left his camping place and headed for the hills. It took him several days to find his way back to the coast again.

After walking westward for many more weeks, Buckley came across a spear sticking out of a mound of earth that looked like a grave. He pulled the spear out and used it as a walking stick. Then, tramping through the bush with the spear in his hand, he came face to face with a tribe of Aborigines – the Wathaurung people.

They took him to their camp and lit a great fire. Then they painted their faces and performed a corroboree. As they chanted and leapt around the fire, poor Buckley feared for his life. But he needn't have worried. The tribe thought this huge white man was their elder, Murrangurk, returned from the dead.

They gave him a possum-skin rug and brought him all their most prized foods: witchetty grubs, yams and roast possum. At night he was given the best hut to sleep in.

The Wathaurung people accepted Buckley into the tribe as an honoured member. He gradually learned their language and their stories about the Dreamtime. They taught him many other things – to hunt for kangaroos with spears, to rub two sticks together to make fire, to cook between hot stones on the campfire, to make canoes out of bark, and much more.

In May 1835, John Batman sailed from Van Diemen's Land to Port Phillip Bay in search of grazing lands. One of his party, William Todd, was left in charge of a small group of men at Indented Head. It was there, on 6 July, that Todd saw a strange figure striding towards the camp – a giant of a man with wild matted hair and a long grey beard. He was draped in possum skins and carried a spear. The strangest part of all was that he was fair-skinned!

Buckley spent many years with the Wathaurung tribe. When they moved to fresh hunting grounds in the Otways area he went with them. But after many more years had passed, he grew tired of wandering about. He wanted to settle down by himself, so he built a bark hut on the banks of Thompson's Creek. From there he could gaze out across the sea. Occasionally, he must have seen sailing ships passing through Bass Strait.

Thirty-two years had passed since Buckley had seen another fellow-countryman. In that time, he had almost forgotten how to speak English. But somehow he managed to find the words to tell his remarkable tale. Then he held out his arm, which was tattooed with his initials: W. B. No one could doubt his story.

Buckley's knowledge of Aboriginal languages and customs was soon put to use by Batman and other members of his party. Buckley was used as an interpreter in dealings between the whites and Aborigines. And he later accompanied Governor Bourke as a guide and interpreter on an inland trip. As a reward for this work, Buckley was granted his freedom.

There he worked as a storekeeper and later as a gatekeeper. But the extraordinary events of his life had changed him forever. The once cheerful and friendly young Buckley had turned into a sad and lonely figure. He could have told many amazing stories of his life as a member of the Wathaurung tribe, but he rarely spoke about those thirty-two long years in the bush.

Buckley survived against all odds and is remembered to this day in the phrase 'Buckley's chance'. This has come to mean almost no chance at all.

But Buckley didn't enjoy his new role in life, so he resigned. In 1837 he sailed for Van Diemen's Land – the place that had filled him with such dread more than thirty years before. By now it was an established colony, with small villages and orderly pasture-lands.

At first, the convicts had no idea where in the world they really were. Some thought China was just to the north, over a large river. Others believed white people lived in a city just beyond the Blue Mountains. Several convicts escaped to try and reach it, but either died in the wilds or returned to captivity.

Many explorers also tried to cross the rugged mountain range, including George Bass, of *Tom Thumb* fame. But all were forced to turn back when faced by sheer towering cliffs.

Then a plague of caterpillars (yes, caterpillars!) ate all the crops and the settlers became desperate to find new grazing pastures for their cattle and land for crops.

Luckily, a farmer called Gregory Blaxland had a brainwave. He studied the routes followed by all the unsuccessful explorers and saw that they had all tried to follow the valleys through the range. He decided to try something completely different…

By the way, do you know why the Blue Mountains are blue? Apparently, it's all to do with all the gumtrees. When light rays are diffused through the drops of eucalypt oil that are constantly being released into the atmosphere a blue colouring is produced.

Well, now you know!

BRYCE COURTENAY

Crossing the Blue Mountains

In 1811, disaster struck the young Colony of New South Wales in the form of a plague of caterpillars. Moving through the settlement's farmlands like a crawling army, the caterpillars destroyed grain crops and grazing country – leaving people, sheep and cattle with little to eat.

The following year a second crisis struck. A harsh drought wiped out even greater areas of grassland, livestock and crops. Meanwhile, shiploads of convicts and free settlers kept arriving – all demanding to be fed.

More grazing land had to be found urgently, or the whole colony would starve to death! But the deep ravines and towering cliffs of the Blue Mountains blocked off all the land to the west. From 1789 onwards, many people had tried to find a way across the rugged mountain range but all had been forced to turn back when faced with the maze of ridges, valleys and sheer cliffs.

Someone, somehow, had to find a way across the forbidding Blue Mountains.

Farmer Gregory Blaxland, an English-born free settler, decided to try. After studying the routes of the other explorers who had attempted the journey, Blaxland hit upon a plan. Instead of walking through the valleys – as many unsuccessful explorers had done – he would climb the main ridge between two rivers, the Grose and the Cox's.

Governor Macquarie gave permission to Blaxland to mount an expedition. On 11 May 1813, Blaxland set off with two other farmers – William Lawson and Charles Wentworth.

They were accompanied by four convicts, five dogs and four horses. The horses were loaded down with ammunition, salted meat, water, flour, tents, axes, a hoe and other necessities.

After crossing the Nepean River the explorers began to climb the steep mountain ridge. The higher they climbed the narrow ridge the more it twisted and turned. One slip, and they could have fallen to their deaths in the deep gullies on either side.

As they climbed higher up the main ridge they struck another problem. Trees and shrubs grew so thickly that it was impossible to keep walking. The men had to stop and hack a path for the horses through the dense bushland. This made the going painfully slow. They only covered about 5 km a day.

After Blaxland and his companions had gone some way they began to cut deep notches on the trees on either side of the track so they could find their way back more easily.

Grass was scarce in this dense bushland, so the horses often went hungry. Whenever the men came to grassy areas they stopped so the horses could graze, and they picked more grass and loaded it onto the horses for future use. Finding water was also a constant problem.

One night, as the explorers sat around their campfire, the dogs began to bark wildly. Something was crashing through the woods. At first the men thought that one of the horses had broken free.

But in the morning they saw footprints and realised they had been surrounded by Aborigines. Blaxland believed that the barking of the dogs had frightened them away. The explorers came across several abandoned shelters and often saw campfires ahead of them, but they never came face to face with the Aborigines.

Almost two weeks after they had first set out the explorers found themselves walking along the top of a mountain, which they named Mount York.

In the late afternoon, they came to a rocky platform and looked out across the country-side. Below them lay a grassy valley through which a river flowed.

By now the horses were so weak the men had to remove their loads. Then they dug a trench down the mountainside to stop the horses slipping and led them down into the valley. There the animals ate and drank their fill and rested until they had regained their strength.

For the next three days the explorers continued westward across the valley. One day they shot a kangaroo and cooked it over the campfire. It made a welcome change from the stale food they had brought with them.

At the end of May the small party came to a mountain which they named Mount Sugarloaf because of its shape. (It was later renamed Mount Blaxland.) When they climbed to its summit they saw just what they had been hoping for – lush grassland as far as the eye could see. Blaxland, Lawson and Wentworth had at last discovered what lay to the west of the mighty Blue Mountains. They were overjoyed!

By now they were running out of food, so Blaxland wisely decided to turn back. They had not quite completed the crossing of the range but they had opened the way for others to follow. On 6 June they crossed the Nepean River back to the settlement. The return trip took just under five days.

Governor Macquarie ordered that a road be built across the mountains. A former army officer, William Cox, was chosen to organise this difficult task. He was put in charge of thirty strong convicts, who finished the job in January 1815. Amazingly, in spite of all the hardships, they had built the road in just six months. They were rewarded for their hard work by being given their freedom, and a small amount of land.

Five months later, Governor Macquarie sent another party, headed by government surveyor George Evans, to go even further west. Using the track carved out by Blaxland, Lawson and Wentworth, Evans and his men reached Mount York in six days. Then they pushed on further west to the country beyond what is now Bathurst. On his return, Evans confirmed that this land was ideal for grazing sheep and cattle.

One of the first to cross the Blue Mountains by carriage was Governor Macquarie, accompanied by his adventurous wife Elizabeth. The Governor wanted to see for himself what lay on the other side of the mountains. He realised that an exciting new chapter in the colony was about to begin.

Blaxland, Lawson and Wentworth were each given 1000 acres (405 hectares) of land. Their heroic feat also earned them an important place in Australian history.

If it wasn't for the discovery of gold we would be a very different nation. Gold brought men and women from all over the world to Australia to seek their fortunes. Many of them decided to stay on and become Australians.

This was a very good thing because now, for the first time, free settlers outnumbered convicts. This meant that our nation could become a society of free people. It wasn't only the gold that made us rich but the golden opportunity to get new people to stay on and become 'us'.

This story is mainly about the Ballarat goldfields, where huge amounts of the precious metal were found, and a very famous rebellion took place. However, rich deposits of gold were found in many other parts of Victoria – and throughout Australia.

The first person to discover an important gold area in Australia was Edward Hargraves. He had gone to the Californian gold rushes and while he was there he noticed that the rock formations were very like those in parts of New South Wales. Maybe he could find gold there! So in January 1851 he returned to Australia to test his theory. He soon struck gold – at Ophir, New South Wales. The rush was on!

Later that year, an even larger goldfield was uncovered near Ballarat, in Victoria.

BRYCE COURTENAY

Gold!

This story begins in 1851 with the discovery of rich gold deposits in the sleepy Buninyong Ranges near Ballarat, Victoria. The news spread like wildfire and in no time thousands of hopeful fortune-hunters were heading for Ballarat. Offices stood empty and ships were marooned in the docks as clerks and ships' crews threw in their jobs and took off for the diggings.

Some came in carts and others on horseback, but most made the long journey from Melbourne on foot, pushing wheelbarrows packed with all the things they needed – from picks, shovels, rifles, tents and blankets to pots, pans and food.

As the news spread further afield, ships full of fortune-hunters began to sail into the port of Melbourne from Germany, Italy, England, Ireland, America, China and many other parts of the world. Australia's greatest gold rush ever had begun!

The once-peaceful Ballarat plains suddenly rang to the sound of axes cutting down ancient gumtrees to line shafts and make other simple mining equipment. Tents were pitched and crude bark huts erected. A tent city sprang up almost overnight. Just three years later, there were almost 20,000 miners on the Ballarat gold-fields.

As soon as the prospectors had pitched their tents they started digging for gold. Some found nuggets just below the surface, but most had to sink shafts deep into the hard earth before striking a reef. This was very hard work. Some didn't find any gold at all and returned home empty-handed.

In those days, Queen Victoria claimed ownership of most of Australia's land. This was known as Crown land, and miners had to pay a government licence to dig on it. The fee was 30 shillings ($3) per month. The diggers felt the fee was far too high, especially as they had to pay it even if they didn't find any gold.

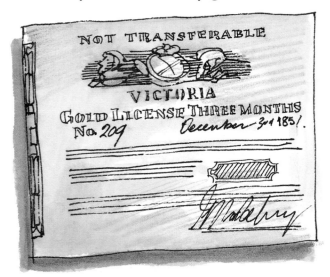

Mounted troopers were sent to check that the diggers had paid their licence fees. These troopers, many of whom were ex-convicts, were often brutal and unreasonable. Sometimes they would force diggers to come up from the depths of their mine shafts just to show their licences. Resentment about the licences grew as the troopers became more and more aggressive. Fights often broke out between troopers and diggers.

In October 1854, a miner was bashed to death at the Eureka Hotel in Ballarat. The publican was charged with his murder, but these charges were later dropped. This angered the diggers because they believed the publican was guilty. They suspected that he'd only got off because he was friendly with the troopers.

So the diggers showed their resentment by burning down his hotel. Several of the miners were then arrested and so was the publican, who was later tried for murder and found guilty. A group of diggers went to see Governor Hotham to demand the release of the arrested miners. This he refused to do.

The following month the diggers held a public meeting at Bakery Hill and formed the Ballarat Reform League. They sent another group of miners to the Governor. This time, they demanded that the government abolish the licence fees. They also asked for the right to vote.

Hotham refused these demands outright. But he realised trouble was brewing, so he sent more soldiers and mounted police to Ballarat to help enforce the law.

71

The angry miners burned their licences and then raised a new flag, the Eureka flag. This featured the Southern Cross and became the symbol of their fight for justice. Irishman Peter Lalor, who was one of the leaders of the rebellion, pointed to the flag and said, "We swear to stand truly by each other, and to fight to defend our rights and liberties." The other miners repeated this. It was known as the Eureka oath.

Then the miners built a barricade from old mining timber and overturned carts. They armed themselves with rifles and gathered inside the stockade. In the early hours of 3 December, just before dawn, the troopers opened fire on the stockade.

Shots rang out from both sides. About 24 miners were killed and 128 taken prisoner. Lalor was shot in the arm, but was helped to safety by some friends. Four troopers fell in the crossfire.

Thirteen miners were charged with high treason, but the charges were later dropped and the men were allowed to go free.

After a government inquiry, the hated monthly licence fee was abolished. It was replaced by a 'miner's right' which cost 1 pound ($2) a year and gave the holder the right to mine for gold and to vote. The miners had at last achieved what they had fought so bravely for! When the news reached the Ballarat goldfields there were great celebrations that lasted well into the night.

Peter Lalor's shattered arm had to be amputated. He went into hiding until the other leaders were cleared and it was safe to come out again. In 1855, he was elected to the Victorian Parliament, where he represented the people of the Ballarat area. He went on to enjoy a long and distinguished parliamentary career.

All the miners who took part in the Eureka Stockade will be remembered for their courage and belief in justice. Some say that this armed rebellion gave birth to true democracy in Australia, and the Eureka flag is seen as a symbol of justice and equality to this day. You can still see its tattered remains in the Ballarat Fine Art Gallery.

Explorers are usually pretty stubborn people. This can be a good thing because it means they're not likely to give up when the going gets tough. Well, Burke was about as stubborn as they come, so he should have been a good explorer.

But, on the other hand, he had no bush experience and he wouldn't listen to others who had. He was also pretty cranky and very impatient and mistrustful. And he did everything in a hurry, regardless of the health of his men. All bad signs for a true explorer and leader.

So, you won't be surprised to hear that things went badly, although he could still have made it home if he'd listened to the Aborigines who wanted to help him. But there you go, some people never learn.

One member of the party, John King, *did* allow the Aborigines to befriend him, and he lived to tell the tale – weak and exhausted though he was.

The famous 'DIG' tree, which is at the heart of this tale of bungling and wasted life, still stands today. So if you're ever in the Cooper Creek area – yes, it's a bit off the beaten track, but you never know – you should go and see it. It really brings the tragic story of Burke and Wills to life.

BRYCE COURTENAY

Burke & Wills

I t was 1860, in the early days of exploration, and the Victorian and South Australian governments were keen to plot a route for a telegraph line across the country. They offered substantial prize money for the first party to cross Australia from south to north — and so the race was on!

But despite the money on offer, only two teams took up the challenge: a Victorian party led by Robert O'Hara Burke, and a South Australian party led by experienced explorer John McDouall Stuart.

The Irish-born Burke had little bush experience. A former soldier, he had migrated to Australia and worked in Victoria as a policeman. But for an expedition of such importance and danger, he was a very unwise choice of leader.

Also in the Victorian party was William John Wills, who was a young surveyor, meteorologist and astronomer. In 1853 Wills had sailed from England to Australia, and worked as a labourer before moving to western Victoria. He soon received an invitation from Burke to join the expedition.

The Royal Society of Victoria had spent two years organising the Victorian expedition and it was the most lavish ever seen in Australia. All in all, the party consisted of 16 men, 24 camels from India, and 24 horses.

They took enough food with them to last for two years, as well as many other supplies, including six tonnes of firewood!

Believing that Stuart's South Australian team had already begun their expedition, Burke's party hastily left Melbourne on 20 August 1860 to a grand send-off from 15,000 well-wishers.

Eager to move on, Burke left the main party behind at Menindee to wait for Wright and took Wills and a small group of men to Cooper's Creek, about halfway between Melbourne and the Gulf of Carpentaria. They had a number of horses and camels with them and provisions for four months. Here Burke waited six weeks for Wright and the others to catch up, but impatience set in and he was reluctant to wait there any longer.

As their journey began, Burke and George Landells, his second-in-command, soon proved to be an ill-matched pair of leaders, arguing frequently. Once they reached Menindee on the Darling River, Burke made Wills second-in-command instead and employed two new men, Charles Gray and William Wright. Wright was to join them in a few weeks.

Burke decided to push ahead with a small supply of food and water and three men – Wills, Gray and King. He left William Brahe in charge of the party at Cooper's Creek, instructing him to wait three months for their return. Foolishly, he left behind the botanist, medical officer and naturalist, all of whom would have been extremely valuable in the bush.

If Burke had waited longer he would have received the news that Stuart's expedition had been abandoned. Had he known this, he could have taken his time and thought things through properly. But that was not to be.

The conditions on the way to the Gulf were rough. Although there was plenty of rainfall, their food supply was meagre and it was extremely hot. Sore and weary, Burke, Wills, Gray and King finally reached the Gulf on 11 February 1861.

But the ever-impatient Burke allowed his team only a day of rest before forcing them on the road to home.

He marched them day and night, even though they were exhausted. Gray fell ill but Burke made him continue.

Hoping that Brahe would still be there, they were bitterly disappointed to find the camp deserted. Their timing was terrible – Brahe and the support party, after waiting four months, had left the site that very morning, just hours before.

For five weeks the explorers struggled on. They finally ran out of food and had to resort to killing two of their animals for food, first a camel, then Burke's horse.

Not long after, on 17 April, Gray died.

Burke, Wills and King took a day to bury him and then set off again, reaching Cooper's Creek three days later.

Brahe had left a small store of food for them – buried at the foot of a tree engraved with 'DIG 3FT NW'. With it was a note in a bottle saying that Brahe's party was mostly well. Burke had almost no hope of catching up to them. He, Wills and King were all unwell and could hardly walk.

Believing they did not have enough supplies to reach Menindie, Burke insisted they make their way instead to Mt Hopeless, where he thought help could be found.

He wrote a note to Brahe, put it in the bottle and in a moment of stupidity buried the bottle again without altering the message carved into the tree.

As Burke's men continued their trek to Mount Hopeless, Aborigines tried to help them but Burke scared them off with gunfire. When the remaining camels died, Burke decided to return to Cooper's Creek and retrace their steps back to Melbourne.

And so it happened that shortly after Burke's party left Cooper's Creek, Brahe and Wright returned there with a final hope of finding the men. But of course they did not find Burke's message, for the campsite looked undisturbed. They assumed the whole party must already be dead.

But Burke and Wills never made it home. Wills became so sick that he insisted the others go on, leaving him in the shade of some branches to die. A few days later Burke also died.

The Aborigines fed and sheltered John King for three months, until a search party finally came.

The fateful 'DIG' tree still stands today, all these years later, marking the tragic site where Burke and Wills died on the banks of Cooper's Creek.

Ned Kelly is one of our biggest folk heroes, which is rather strange because he and his gang robbed banks and shot a few people who got in the way.

But times were different then. The police always seemed to side with the rich and there was very little justice for the poor. So Ned and the Kelly Gang decided they'd take from the rich and get a bit of their own back.

Although there was a reward for their capture, the poor people didn't dob him in because they knew he was on their side. Some people think he was Australia's Robin Hood because he gave a lot of the money to the poor. Other people think he was just another crook.

Whatever the truth is, he still continues to fascinate people. He's been the subject of dozens of books and paintings and several ballads and films.

Kelly himself believed he was the victim of police harassment. After the famous Jerilderie hold-up he stopped to write a very long letter which explained what happened on the day he and Dan first took to the bush. He hoped it would be published in the local paper the next day, and would at last put his side of the story to the public.

But as it turned out the 'Jerilderie Letter' wasn't printed for another 60 years.

BRYCE COURTENAY

Ned Kelly & His Gang

Ned Kelly was born in 1856 in the Victorian country town of Wallan. One of eight children, he lived with his widowed mother in a tumbledown-shack. The Kellys were among many poor Irish families trying to scratch out a living in the area. Like many Irish people, the Kellys hated the English who had taken over Ireland. The Kellys also disliked the police because they believed they picked on the poor and sided with the wealthy. Ned and his brothers were always in trouble with the law – usually for stealing horses and cattle. When he was only 14, Ned was sent to gaol for striking a man. He was back in gaol again at the age of 16 for stealing a horse.

The police offered a reward for the arrest of the Kelly brothers. In the meantime they arrested Mrs Kelly for 'attempted murder of a policeman'. She was sentenced to three years' gaol. The unfairness of this infuriated Ned Kelly and hardened his hatred of the police. The Kelly boys were joined by two mates they had met in gaol, Steve Hart and Joe Byrne. They became known as the Kelly Gang.

In April 1878 Constable Fitzpatrick came to the Kelly house to arrest Ned's brother Dan for horse-stealing. No one is sure of what happened next. According to the Kelly family, Fitzpatrick insulted Ned's sister Kate and a scuffle followed. Then Fitzpatrick's gun accidentally went off, wounding his own wrist. But according to Constable Fitzpatrick, Ned was the one who shot him. Whatever the truth of it, Ned and Dan knew there would be trouble so they took off for the hills.

The gang managed to hide out in the Wombat Mountains, living as bushrangers for a few months. But in October 1878 they came face to face with a party of four policemen at Stringybark Creek. The police drew their guns and so did the bushrangers.

In the gunfight that followed three of the police were shot dead. The fourth, Constable Macintryre, managed to leap onto his horse and raise the alarm at Mansfield police station. But the gang was far away by the time they returned.

After resting, dining and feeding their horses, three members of the gang rode into the nearby township of Euroa and held up the bank, taking the manager, his family and staff prisoner. They removed nearly two thousand pounds ($4000) from the safe, then put their prisoners into carts and drove them out to the farm. At nightfall the gang galloped off into the bush. They later shared the money with their family and friends, paying off fines and debts.

The Kelly Gang were declared outlaws, wanted for murder. The Victorian government offered a reward of one thousand pounds ($2000) for each member of the gang – dead or alive. Despite the reward, Ned Kelly and his gang managed to evade the police for almost two years. But they didn't always lie low. In fact, they were soon to carry out two robberies that had the whole country talking.

Two months after the shooting Kelly and his gang held up a farmer and his family, keeping them prisoner for two days.

The following February the Kelly Gang struck again. This time they crossed the border to Jerilderie in New South Wales. Arriving at midnight, they went to the police station and roused the policemen from their beds. Then they locked them in their own cells! Next morning, the gang put on police uniforms and herded everyone in town into the Royal Hotel.

Meanwhile, Ned Kelly and Joe Byrne held up the bank, again taking about two thousand pounds. Kelly burned all the mortgages in the safe. Now there was no record of how much money all the poor farmers owed to the bank. Then, at gunpoint, they forced the staff of the bank to cross the road to the Royal Hotel.

Before leaving town, the Kelly Gang cut the telegraph wires, so news of the robbery could not get out. The gang took to the mountain country where they managed to hide from the police for more than a year. By now they were heroes to some members of the public, especially to the poor people who felt the laws favoured the rich. People made up popular songs and ballads glorifying the daring Kelly Gang and ridiculing the police.

The police, who were by now desperate to catch the gang, retaliated by doubling the reward for their capture, but even this didn't help. People lied to the police and helped to cover the Kelly Gang's tracks. Some people even gave them food and shelter.

But the reward was too tempting for one man: Aaron Sherritt. An old horse-stealing friend of the gang, he began to give information to the police. After a while the gang grew suspicious of

their friend. So they set a trap for him. They told him they were heading for a certain spot, and when the police turned up at that place the gang knew that Sherritt was a traitor.

When Ned Kelly heard that the Victorian police had brought some Aboriginal trackers down from Queensland he knew that time was running out. He realised that the Aboriginal trackers would have no trouble finding him and his gang. So Kelly hatched his most desperate plan yet. He decided it was time to lead the police to the small Victorian town of Glenrowan for a shoot-out.

But first there was another score to settle. Joe Byrne and Dan Kelly went to Aaron Sherritt's house and knocked on the door. When he opened it they shot him dead. Then they rode back to Glenrowan.

While Joe Byrne and Dan Kelly had been at Aaron Sherritt's house, Ned Kelly and Steve Hart had forced some railway workers to tear up tracks leading to the township of Glenrowan. They knew that when news of Sherritt's shooting reached Melbourne a train-load of police and Aboriginal trackers would be heading for the township – and they wanted that train derailed.

The gang rounded up the people of Glenrowan and held them prisoner in Jones's Hotel while they waited for the train to arrive. They threw a party in the inn, chatting to their prisoners and urging them to enjoy themselves. They even showed the townsfolk the strange armour they had made from iron plates. It was very heavy but bullet-proof.

Among the prisoners was the town's school-master, Mr Curnow. He asked Ned Kelly for per-mission to take his family home. Kelly said he could, as long as he didn't go for help.

At last, in the early hours of Monday morning, the Kelly Gang heard a steam train whistle. They rushed out, expecting to hear a crash, but instead the train ground slowly to a halt. Curnow had managed to signal the train to stop before it reached the broken rails. He had then told the police where to find the gang.

The siege of Glenrowan was about to begin. Ned Kelly came out of the hotel in his armour. Shots rang out. He was shot in the arm and foot but he managed to stagger up into the bush behind the hotel. The other three members of the gang were still inside. By now the hotel was surrounded by police.

Bullets flew back and forth. Some people managed to escape outside. Then, just as it began to grow light, a tall armoured figure lurched through the mist, firing with his only good hand. Ned Kelly had returned to save the other members of his gang. Bullets bounced off his chest but then he was shot in the legs – and down he fell. Ned Kelly was caught at last!

Joe Byrne had been shot in the siege. Dan Kelly and Steve Hart were still alive but refused to surrender. After letting the remaining townspeople run out, the police set fire to the hotel. Dan Kelly and Hart died in the blaze.

Ned Kelly survived his many gunshot injuries. He was tried for the murder of the policemen at Stringybark Creek and found guilty. Ned Kelly he was hanged at the Melbourne Gaol on 11 November 1880. His last words were, "Such is life!" He was 24 years old.